I am a DOLPHIN

Steve Macleod

www.av2books.com

Go to **www.av2books.com**, and enter this book's unique code.

BOOK CODE

L808774

AV² by **Weigl** brings you media enhanced books that support active learning.

AV² provides enriched content that supplements and complements this book. Weigl's AV² books strive to create inspired learning and engage young minds in a total learning experience.

Your AV² Media Enhanced books come alive with...

Audio
Listen to sections of the book read aloud.

Video
Watch informative video clips.

Embedded Weblinks
Gain additional information for research.

Try This!
Complete activities and hands-on experiments.

Key Words
Study vocabulary, and complete a matching word activity.

Quizzes
Test your knowledge.

Slide Show
View images and captions, and prepare a presentation.

... and much, much more!

Published by AV² by Weigl
350 5th Avenue, 59th Floor New York, NY 10118
Website: www.av2books.com www.weigl.com

Macleod, Steve.
Dolphin / Steve Macleod.
     p. cm. -- (I am)
  ISBN 978-1-61690-754-9 (hardcover : alk. paper) -- ISBN 978-1-61690-761-7 (softcover : alk. paper)
1. Dolphins--Juvenile literature. I. Title.
  QL737.C432M24 2011
  599.53--dc22

                          2010052408

Printed in the United States of America in North Mankato, Minnesota
1 2 3 4 5 6 7 8 9 0 15 14 13 12 11

052011
WEP37500

Project Coordinator: Aaron Carr Art Director: Terry Paulhus

Weigl acknowledges Getty Images as the primary image supplier for this title.

I AM A DOLPHIN

In this book, I will teach you about

- **myself**
- **my food**
- **my home**
- **my family**

and much more!

3

I am a dolphin.

4

I can hold my breath
for more than 10 minutes.

I use sound to see.

8

I make up to 1,000 clicking noises every second.

11

I learn a special whistle
and use it as my name.

13

I can jump higher than a house.

I can swim when
I am sleeping.

I swallow my food without chewing.

I live in water
where fishers work.

I am a dolphin.

DOLPHIN FACTS

This page provides more detail about the interesting facts found in the book. Simply look for the corresponding page number to match the fact.

Pages 4-5

I am a dolphin. Dolphins live in oceans all around the world. They have long, sleek bodies, with flippers to help them swim. A curved mouth on their snout makes dolphins look like they are smiling. Dolphins are also known for their intelligence.

Pages 6–7

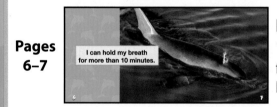

Dolphins can hold their breath for more than 10 minutes. Most people can only hold their breath underwater for less than one minute. Dolphins rise to the surface of the water to breathe air through a hole in the top of their head.

Pages 8–9

Dolphins use sound to see. They make clicking sounds that travel through water. When the sounds hit something, an echo bounces back to the dolphin. From the echo, the dolphin can determine the distance, size, and shape of objects.

Pages 10–11

Dolphins make up to 1,000 clicking noises every second. Compare that to the world's fastest talking female, who can speak 11 words per second. Dolphins communicate using many other sounds, too. They can make squeals, clicks, pops, yelps, and whistles.

Pages 12–13

Dolphins learn a special whistle and use it as their name. Scientists call this a "signature whistle." It is thought that dolphins use this whistle to tell each other who they are. Dolphins learn their signature whistle by the time they are one year old.

Pages 14–15

Dolphins can jump higher than a house. Dolphins can jump 16 feet (4.9 meters) out of the water. That is about the same height as a one-story house. In nature, scientists believe dolphins jump to save energy while traveling or to catch fish. Some dolphins even do tricks in the air.

Pages 16–17

Dolphins can swim when they are sleeping. This light sleep is similar to when people take a nap. When dolphins take their naps, they will swim slowly next to another animal. Dolphins can also sleep while lying still.

Pages 18–19

Dolphins swallow their food without chewing. They only use their teeth for catching food. Dolphins have three parts to their stomach. They use all three parts to help digest their food because they swallow it whole.

Pages 20–21

Dolphins live in water where fishers work. This is dangerous because dolphins can become tangled in fishing nets and equipment, and die. Scientists have a hard time estimating the exact number of dolphins in the world. They are considered a protected species.

WORD LIST

Research has shown that as much as 65 percent of all written material published in English is made up of 300 words. These 300 words cannot be taught using pictures or learned by sounding them out. They must be recognized by sight. This book contains 32 common sight words to help young readers improve their reading fluency and comprehension. This book also teaches young readers several important content words, such as proper nouns. These words are paired with pictures to aid in learning and improve understanding.

Page	Sight Words
4	a, am, I
6	can, for, hold, I, more, my, ten, than
8	I, see, to, use
10	every, I, make, second, to, up
12	a, and, as, I, it, my, name, use
14	a, can, I, high, house, jump, than
16	am, can, I, sleep, when
18	food, I, my
20	a, am, I, in, live, water, where, work

Page	Content Words
4	dolphin
6	breath, minute
8	sound
10	click, noise
12	learn, special, whistle
14	
16	swim
18	chew, swallow, without
20	dolphin, fisher

24